**Museum für
Kunsthandwerk**

Phaidon Press Ltd
140 Kensington Church Street
London W8 4BN

First published 1992

©1992, Phaidon Press Limited

ISBN 0 7148 2765 7

A CIP catalogue record for this book is available from
the British Library

Acknowledgements: The author is very grateful to
Richard Meier and members of his office, particularly Lisa Green, who so patiently answered many
questions and provided so much material; to Dr
Annaliese Ohm, the first director, who spent a
great deal of time explaining the museum and its
early history; to Dr Arnulf Herbst, the present
director, who talked about its current working; to
Ursula Seitz-Gray who took the photographs; and
to Oliver Ralphs who redrew the constructional
drawings with great care.

Printed and bound in Hong Kong

Museum für Kunsthandwerk
Richard Meier

MICHAEL BRAWNE

1

Light and the museum

At one point during the design stage of the Museum für Kunsthandwerk Richard Meier needed a photograph of the site. A photographer in Frankfurt – Ursula Seitz-Gray – was commissioned to take some views into which photographs of the model could be photomontaged. As she was about to take the pictures there was an unexpected snow-shower and then no time in which to take another set before Meier's arrival in Frankfurt. Seitz-Gray apologized for the mishap but, to her surprise, Richard Meier was delighted; the white model against a white background was of course exactly the white on white Suprematist image which was one of the roots of this design and indeed of much of his architecture.

What the photomontage would have shown is a group of cubicular forms, three new, one old, by the River Main, each cube linked to the other in some way so that the whole was a legible unity yet each element recognizable as an entity; each white on the outside but also on the inside; white within white.

The purpose of those cubes was to house a collection of objects which, if one were to make minute distinctions, were from the upper levels of the applied arts. They were only distinguished from what is often spuriously labelled as fine art by actually having a utilitarian purpose: furniture, carpets, china, glass, metalwork, from Europe, the countries of Islam and the Far East. Hardly any were large and most of

them had been part of the domestic environment of palaces or the houses of the wealthy. It was not a collection of folk art; that would be displayed in another museum further along the embankment. All therefore seemed to fit the notion of being placed within a villa-like museum that was part of a new museum quarter in one of the richest cities in the world. Place, concept and contents seemed to mesh. As did, most crucially, the ideas of the architect and the director.

The design of museums represents a most serious paradox: light is the essential element which makes it possible for us to see the objects yet in a very large number of instances that light damages those objects. This is true even for a collection containing pieces made for ordinary reasonably-lit interiors. Carpets, textiles and painted wood, for instance, all suffer deterioration under the action of light. The damage is proportional to the intensity of illumination and to the length of exposure. The demands of conservation therefore often suggest weakly-lit exhibition areas. These are most readily achieved by relying on controllable artificial lighting.

Yet whiteness demands luminosity; the play of sun on surfaces. No doubt Richard Meier would endorse Louis Kahn's statement that 'no space, architecturally, is a space unless it has natural light'. Kahn solved that paradox at the Kimbell in Fort Worth and at the Yale Center for British Art, **2**, at New Haven (opposite his earlier university art gallery) in ways

which are both magical and effective. Meier took another but equally successful route at Frankfurt.

At the Center for British Art Kahn had recognized that not all parts of a museum need have highly-controlled light levels. The entrance hall or circulation spaces without exhibits, for example, could have much more generous daylight – could even allow the sun to enter. Two internal covered courts provide both a focus and a zone in which less controlled daylight is permitted to play on timber walls and can be seen to do so from openings in the top-floor gallery.

Meier translates these central almost classic courtyards of a palazzo into the more dynamic forms of a ramp and a layered arrangement of walls that gradually temper the light of the outside so that the gallery spaces can in fact have levels which are acceptable in terms of conservation. But the openings in the wall, as in Kahn's building, always allow a view of the more brightly-lit areas and thus powerfully reinforce the sense of a space primarily lit by natural light.

Most of the galleries also have windows. These are of course an essential element of the external composition, since they turn a plain cubicular volume into a series of inhabited floors at the scale of a villa; they relate the building to the existing villa on the site and to the neighbourhood. Internally they allow a view out but because the light still needs to be controlled, blinds of a grey plastic cloth can be raised and lowered as required. The view through the

2

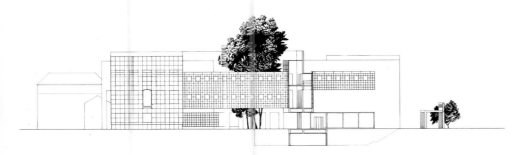

fine mesh of the old part of Frankfurt on the other side of the river is of a town seen on a dull misty day, which somehow does not help the exhibits or the room. Perhaps the solution is too simple and some more subtle filtering through layering – as elsewhere – could have dealt with the conflicting demands of outside and inside more successfully. The windows also have the effect of pushing the exhibits into the middle of the room, especially as the amount of wall left between the windows is insufficient for most objects. The reconciliation of the demands of the inside and outside is one of the perennial problems of architecture and again particularly relevant now that we have abandoned the naive belief that the exterior is simply an expression of the forces shaping the interior, which had at one time been an avowed tenet of modern architecture.

Precedents

The work of Richard Meier is deeply rooted in that architecture of the 1920s and 1930s which we associate with Le Corbusier, with the white international style of Garche, 3 or the Villa Savoye 4. But that rootedness is not one of simply mimicking the work of the master but one of understanding how the work of Le Corbusier (or for that matter that of any other great architect) could be the beginning and not necessarily the culmination of a tradition. It is to recognize greatness as a source of inspiration; to look upon Le Corbusier as generations of architects in Europe and North America looked upon Palladio, with immensely fruitful results.

Meier initially shared that view with four other American architects – Peter Eisenmann, Michael Graves, Charles Gwathmey and John Hejduk – who became known as the 'New York Five'. Only Meier however has remained true to the original idea and continues to pursue it to this day adding a new and important complexity. His design for the J. Paul Getty Center high above Los Angeles due for completion in 1995, for example, stems from the same roots as his Frankfurt museum.

We associate this white architecture with industrial production and the forms of the machine not least, of course, because Le Corbusier told us to do so in *Vers une Architecture*. It could therefore be argued that an architecture with such overtones is perhaps an inappropriate setting for works crafted by hand. The Museum für Kunsthandwerk is after all, as its name implies, for works of art done by hand. It is not a museum of design. Equally there is a frequent association between this architecture and the rational; a belief that it represents a clinically clean cool approach far removed from the realms of art. Both notions are based on serious misconceptions.

First, objects taken out of their original setting and placed in a museum acquire a new and necessarily different reality, that of the museum environment.

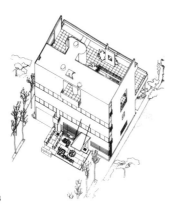

3

4

6

That this setting needs to have sympathy with the objects, to be in scale with them for example, is not in question. It cannot possibly however repeat the original surroundings in their entirety; if it tries too hard it is likely to fail like a trite rhyme. As Richard Meier wrote in the publication which accompanied the opening of the museum in 1985 'Architecture defers to the exhibits, serving as a frame for their display'. That frame has a validity of its own. Perhaps its most important attribute is that it should qualitatively approach the level of the exhibits.

The second misconception is that the machine is the antithesis of the romantic. For Le Corbusier and many architects of his generation the machine, partly precisely because of its apparent rationality, was an object of intensely romantic feelings. It was to be a great liberating force and the root of a profound optimism in the future. The photographs of cars and aeroplanes in *Vers une Architecture* are among the most romantic images in the book.

The buildings designed by Meier before he started on the Frankfurt building are equally imbued with such a romantic sense. The Douglas House, 5, 6, of 1971–73 on its steep wooded hillside, or the Atheneum, 7, a visitor centre in New Harmony, Indiana of 1975–79 rising above a long lawn, are great white forms of a complex geometry – pure forms displaced and moulded – against nature, a tradition which has come down to us from the Greeks.

The architectural competition

The awareness of these earlier buildings and perhaps a view that something similar might be appropriate for a European museum led to the invitation in 1979 to participate in a limited competition. The other competitors were Robert Venturi and Denise Scott-Brown Hans Hollein from Austria and four groups from the Federal Republic: Hollzinger and Goepfert, Heinz Mohl, Novotny and Mahner and Tritt and Quast. The competitors met in Frankfurt on 9 November 1979 for an open question and answer session with the judges, an arrangement which makes at least some form of architect/client relationship possible even in a competition.

Meier's building did not immediately take the form which was eventually built. Sketches, 8, of early December show a much more unified square form which was at first detached from the villa on the site and then later subsumed it as part of a closure of a curved courtyard. Two sketches, both dated 12 December 1979, give the first clear indication of the division into four identifiable elements and the displacement of the grid, as well as the axial lines of the garden layout.

These lines, the dimensions of the villa and the 3 5° displacement are important clues to the design and in a sense control the entire development both horizontally and vertically. The components of the moves which were made at the time are set out

7

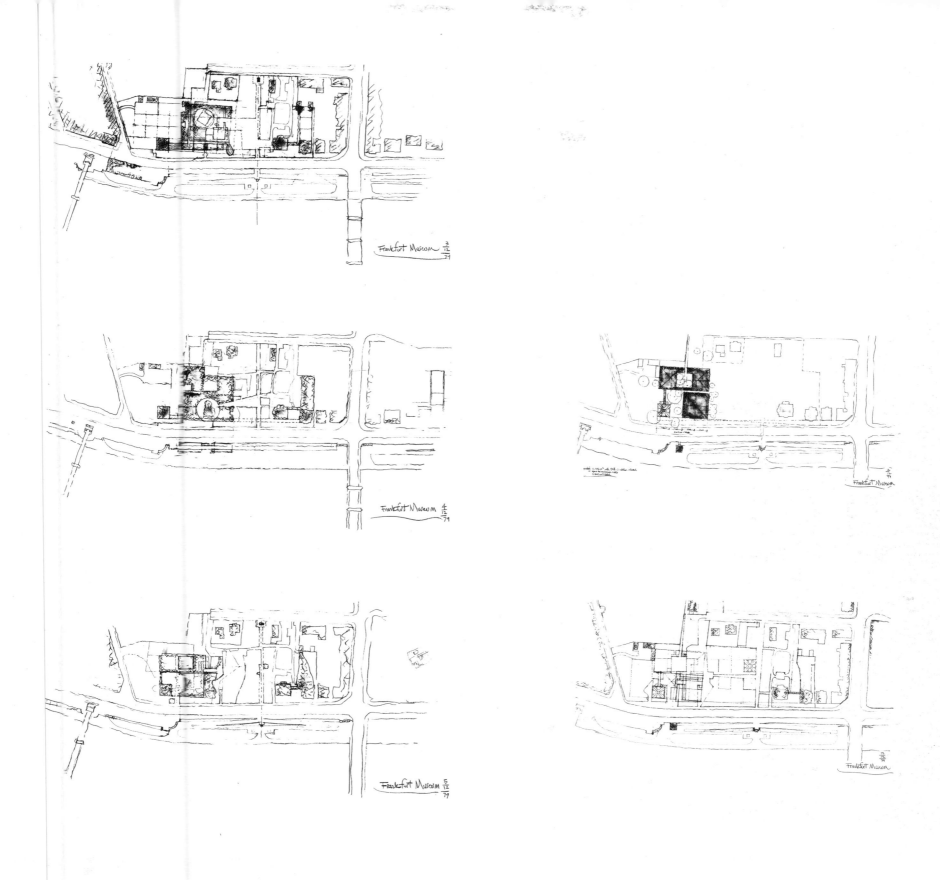

Frankfurt Museum 3/12/79

Frankfurt Museum 4/12/79

Frankfurt Museum 5/12/79

8 Richard Meier, sketches made
between 3rd and 12th December 1979
during the competition stage.

in five diagrams, **9**, each including a description produced by Meier. They demonstrate quite clearly the interaction between the building and the urban concerns which were seen as important. They are a very particular answer to a specific location, and are, for example, significantly different from the later Post Museum by Günter Behnisch, slightly down river, which was opened in September 1990 and which also has to relate to a villa. It does so in a much more dramatic and dynamic manner; the relationship is much less precise, much less classically urban.

The competition entries were to be submitted on 31 January 1980 and the jury met on 25 and 26 April 1980. It was chaired by Josef Paul Kleihues who has since designed the Museum for Pre- and Early History in Frankfurt, part of the amazing museum building programme which has occurred in the city during the last 15 years. The first prize was awarded unanimously by the jury of nine members to Richard Meier; the second prize was divided equally between Venturi, Rauch, Scott-Brown and Hans Hollein.

Six months later, on 28 October 1980, the city commissioned Richard Meier to go ahead with the planning of the museum. By March 1981 the main design stage was complete and it was possible to prepare cost estimates which amounted to DM 43.7 million. In November 1981 the city council formally approved the building of the museum and on 1 March 1982 there was a ceremony to mark the digging of the first sod. A little over two years later, in August

1984, the main areas of the building were ready for the installation of the display and the placing of the collections. The formal opening of the museum took place on 25 April 1985, roughly seven years after the city of Frankfurt had first asked its Building Department to consider this project.

The whole project was monitored by a group from the city's Building Department led by Roland Burgard which also exercised control of cost and construction schedules. They laid down as a guiding principle that cost took priority over time. In line with this the following schedule was devised:

'Conclusion of carcass work including roofing within one calendar year. In the case in question this had the following advantages: work could begin, and the excavation of the site could be completed before the maximum ground-water level was reached in early summer, the reinforced-concrete work could be carried out quickly during the warm season, and, once the roof skin had been applied in December, the installation of the ventilation ducts and the sanitary fittings could be started before winter really set in. The remaining carcass work could be completed before the trade unions held their next rounds of tariff meetings the following May. About eighteen months would then be available for fitting the building out.'

All the architectural drawings were done in the office of Richard Meier & Partners in New York so that day-

to-day control could be exercised and decisions made on the spot by those ultimately responsible for the building. The drawings are lettered in German and dimensions given in metric units. The specialist consultants – structural engineers, environmental control engineers, lighting engineers, acousticians, exterior wall specialists and so on – all had offices in Frankfurt or nearby. The whole process before and during construction was co-ordinated at project meetings in Frankfurt which took place at three-weekly intervals and which were primarily attended by a German architect, Günter Standke, who had come to work in Richard Meier's office not long before and who became the partner in charge of the project.

Methods of construction

The white architecture of the 1920s and 1930s has not survived the rigours of the weather or the neglect of the war years very successfully, not because it was white, since colour, frequently strong colour, played an important role, but because of the way it was constructed. The Villa Savoye, for instance, was wrecked by German occupying troops. It has since been carefully repaired and restored but still shows signs of being unable to cope with the vagaries of the weather and the movement which so often results. What is clearly needed is a different

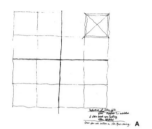

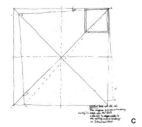

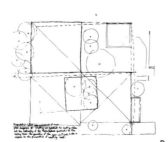

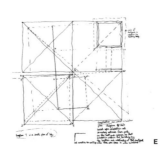

Richard Meier, five diagrams which analyse the structural and organizational development of the design.

A The location on the site of the cubic form of the Villa Metzler, locations of the existing trees. Retaining all of the buildings on the site suggested a building responsive to these conditions.

B The organizational grid of the Museum extension incorporates the Villa Metzler as one quadrant of a square plan. Its modulation is based upon a replication of the basic form and dimensions of the Villa.

C A 3½° displacement of a portion of the building is necessary to obtain a frontal relationship with the facades of all of the other existing museums along the Schaumainkai to the west.

D The skewed walkway made by the 3½° shift of the grid reflects the pedestrian route from Metzlerstrasse to Schaumainkai and the Eiserner Steg.

E the intersection of the pedestrian crosswalks produces a fragmentation of the original grid and the creation of an open courtyard based on the diagonal grid.

12

10

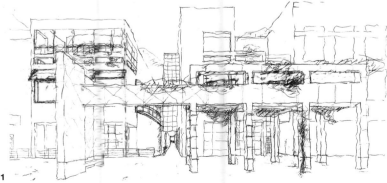

11

technology, a new way of constructing buildings which makes them more robust but which nevertheless allows the creation of white forms and especially of forms which will remain white.

Early modern architecture required unbroken planes in order to emphasize its cubicular intentions and to avoid joints which might in some way suggest traditional materials like stone or timber. It is in the nature of buildings, however, to move and adjust between day and night, summer and winter. Overlapping slates or tiles on a roof, for example, do this with ease.

The process which made a permanent white surface possible was that of porcelain enamelling. Glass frit is fused to steel panels at very high temperatures and provides a coating which, if it is not chipped, is extremely long lasting. Glass is after all, an inert material which has survived intact for 2000 years; Roman glass looks as it did when it was made.

There are, however, limits to the size of the steel panels both in terms of manufacture and ease of erection. Those on the museum are 1.10m × 1.10m. Significantly they are square like the subdivisions of the windows and the mesh on the balustrades, 10, 11, but perhaps also to take them away from any association with masonry. The panels are, or course much more like hung tiles; a thin outer shield that provides a protective cladding of the desired colour.

A good deal of the exterior is covered in these panels but by no means all. There are sizeable areas of stucco. This render is, however, not applied directly onto masonry or concrete but onto a 50mm layer of insulation. This outer layer keeps the material behind it in a stable condition and is itself much less likely to move than a masonry wall.

Much of the base of the building where both stucco and porcelain enamelled panels are too vulnerable is clad in Sarizzo-Antigorio, an Italian granite which also echoes the base of the Villa Metzler, the original building on the site.

The windows have lacquered aluminium frames made from large hollow extrusions which are triple-glazed. Several, particularly those at the side of the ramp, also have external blinds which fit into a recess above the window frame.

This combination of new techniques makes the development and continuation of the architecture of the modern movement possible in ways which weren't available half a century or so earlier. Similarly the development of movable platforms, raised and lowered pneumatically, makes it much easier to carry out cleaning and maintenance of the facade on a regular basis. A visitor to the building may come across a whole crew and their yellow platform washing windows, panels and dirt-collecting ledges. Such a programme of cleaning the face of the building must be seen by architect and client as part of the design.

The setting for the display

The competition concitions made clear the intentions of the museum director and her colleagues as far as the display of objects was concerned. These were, in her own words:

'to achieve, primarily, the permanent exhibition of the museum's possessions. The presentation of all exhibits made of the most varied materials will be arranged chronologically and grouped according to artistic and regional affiliations… It can be assumed that no basically different system of arranging the exhibits will be introduced. A museum of arts and crafts will always require small, compact spaces… In accordance with their nature, the exhibits call for a conception of space based on small units. Walls of room height that create spaces are to be preferred to partitions or suspended walls.'

The spatial organization could have simply continued the room plans of the Villa Metzler, **14 (overleaf)**, or created a series of enfiladed galleries as in the traditional museum plan. Neither would have been quite right. The villa repeated another three times would have been banal and would have prevented the sense of occasion created by the entry and circulation spaces. Enfiladed rooms would have been too reminiscent of the standard picture gallery.

13

What was needed was a sequence of domestic-sized areas which were both part of the flow of space, of the movement of visitors, which allowed contact with the outside, **13**, and provided the kind of definition and enclosure which was in scale with the objects on view. What was also desirable was a sense of permanence – what was probably being adversely criticized by the use of the words 'partitions or suspended walls' was that flimsy feeling of so many museum installations. The solution was to create a varied arrangement of thick walls – over 800mm in width as a rule – within each major space, which became a background or could be hollowed out for showcases or niches and which were also often linked by beams which framed an opening or defined an object on a platform. It was an architectural organization of substance which stood within each structural space. These walls are made of a light metal framework clad in particle board and are, therefore, actually and hierarchically less permanent than the building; they can be changed at some future date.

The visual sequence which results is that we sense the major space defined by wall and columns, then the order of smaller rooms within this space and finally objects on platforms or within showcases, **15**. The case or niche is the smallest enclosure, a room within a room within a room, which can also be defined still further by choosing an individual background colour that relates to its contents.

14

The spatial gradation is like that of the stacking Russian dolls that diminish progressively but always fit within each other. But because, unlike the dolls, we see the whole sequence at once, occasionally the museum looks empty; the figure/ground relationship gives too much emphasis to the background. The same rooms filled with vibrant Yves Klein or Rothko paintings would in no way even hint at such a problem.

Although the sense of daylight pervades many of the rooms, most exhibits are mainly lit by artificial light and especially of course in those areas where objects liable to be damaged by excessive natural light are on display. The system used is what might now be described as an almost standard solution: recessed downlighters for general illumination, including all the circulation areas and recessed track, in the ceiling in the display galleries to which simple white cylindrical fittings are attached.

The showcases are internally lit by fittings behind a very fine layer of flattened wire louvres which was originally developed as a material which would act as both sunshade and insect screen. It is visually much less coarse than the more usual eggcrate louvre. What is important, however, is that these sources – with very few exceptions – are incandescent and therefore at the red end of the visible spectrum. They are thus much more like the light we associate with domestic interiors.

The resolution of the interior was strongly affected by discussions with the director, Dr Annaliese Ohm who held firm views about the character of a museum of applied art. Even at the competition stage she had favoured Richard Meier's design so that there was never a question of an architectural jury forcing a design on a reluctant client. From the start there was a sympathy as well as a recognition that both architecture and contents have meaning and that each has a role to play in the total experience of the visitor.

From the beginning Dr Ohm had very specific views as to what was not wanted: a dark box of undifferentiated space in the name of flexibility, a theatrical display totally introverted, an enclosed space with different colours for different sections which fragmented the building. What she felt was needed was intimacy, rooms of about 300m² within which small objects could be seen in natural light; that the sense of the domestic could still be emphasized within the context of a museum. Richard Meier's design exceeded her expectations and she holds that five years after its completion and with a new director – and therefore no doubt with different attitudes – the museum still works extremely well. It does so in the case of the permanent display as well as the frequent temporary exhibitions which are held in the daylit ground-floor gallery at the foot of the ramp, and in the darker Graphics gallery on the second floor.

15

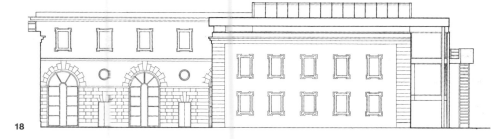

The role of models

The design of the Museum für Kunsthandwerk was started at the end of 1979; that for the High Museum in Atlanta, Georgia, also by Richard Meier, was started in 1980, 16. The High was finished in 1984, a year before the completion of the Frankfurt building, so the two projects ran very much in parallel. They obviously share a number of features beyond the characteristic handwriting of their architect. In the work of any architect – Le Corbusier, Kahn or Meier – earlier designs become models for later ones: partly perhaps because there is a natural inclination to build on known success, mainly no doubt because there are inevitable visual preferences and therefore a limited set of forms from which a selection is made.

Both in Frankfurt and Atlanta there is a separation of the main vertical circulation from the galleries which allows a celebration of that movement. In each case it is dramatic and a key element of the building. In Frankfurt it is outward looking, a link to the river and the city, in Atlanta it is a ramp which overlooks an inward-facing top-lit court. At each level the galleries are beyond this court which, although on the periphery, appears as a central space. The difference may partly be a reflection of the site – the High Museum is just off an ordinary tree-lined street – but it may also be a response to the need in American museums to have a large gathering place for the frequent social events

associated with fund raising. Whatever the reason, the effect is significant.

The exterior is made of very much the same materials and appears as a set of white forms in a green park. The forms are however more loosely disposed and are very much more windowless. They are certainly not reminiscent of an inhabited villa and indeed have to relate to quite bulky neighbouring structures; one side of the High shares a terrace with one of the entrances to the Robert W. Woodruff Art Center.

In 1982, while work was going on in Frankfurt and Atlanta, Richard Meier started to design an addition to the Des Moines Art Center, 17. This consisted of three separate components, each attached to the original building designed by Eliel Saarinen in 1948, the whole woven together in a less regulated manner than at Frankfurt.

Frankfurt was, moreover, not Meier's first essay in museum design. He came to it with a long-standing interest in the display of art, a preoccupation which he shares with virtually every significant architect of this century. The interest first found expression in a project for the Museum of Modern Art at the Villa Strozzi in Florence in 1973, 18. Richard Meier produced a design for the stables and their courtyard interlacing new with old. The first realization of a space for art occurred in 1977 with an installation for The New York School exhibition at the State Museum in Albany, New York, a series of rooms

16

17

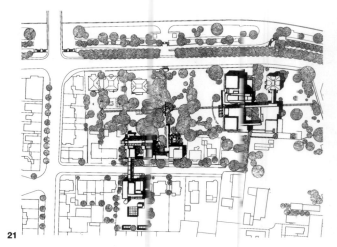

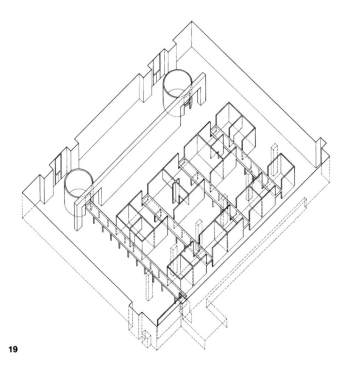

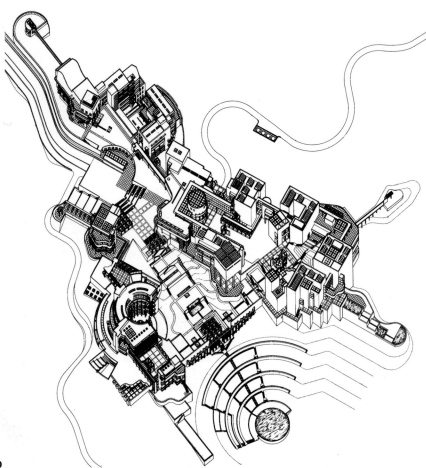

defined by walls and columns, **19**. In each case the poetic complexity so evident in Frankfurt can also be felt in these designs. Many of the strands which are visible in this series of buildings are likely to come together in the Getty Center, **20**, – a kind of arts campus on a promontory above Santa Monica Bay – when it is completed in 1995.

The connection will be most immediately visible when Meier's project for the Ethnology Museum (Museum für Völkerkunde) is completed within the same urban block in Frankfurt, **21**. Construction is due to start in 1991. The geometry and garden layout for the first museum will in fact only fully come into their own when the second slightly larger design – also composed of white cubes and free planes – becomes visible through the dense trees of the park. It will be the latest in a remarkable series of 13 new museums which has been created in Frankfurt in the last ten years along, on, or at least near, the banks of the Main. The fact that Meier has been responsible for two of these 13 can be taken as a tribute to the undoubted popularity of his Kunsthandwerk Museum in the city.

The legacy

Buildings can be seen and understood as isolated creations, as events that occur at a particular moment. But they can also, and probably more fruitfully, be considered as a sequence in the work of any architect which in turn immediately creates a legacy for others to follow. One of the early starting points for Richard Meier was, after all, just that assumption. As practising architects we are not only interested in the original source but also in what flowed from it; in a sense, how fruitful it can be, so that however fundamental the work of Palladio is in the history of Palladianism, for instance, the buildings of Robert Adam or Colen Campbell or Thomas Jefferson are also of significance in terms of its world-wide legacy. The idea of some sense of historical continuity is crucial to our understanding in general, but probably particularly so in the case of the museum in Frankfurt.

What the sequence of projects described perhaps shows is a deep-seated preoccupation with an architecture which can best be described as baroque. It is a pursuit of a geometrically-ordered complexity, not usually instantly understood, which goes hand in hand with the manipulation of light on reflecting surfaces. Although perhaps in one way mysterious it is at the same time joyful and optimistic. The tradition which is being explored has its roots as much, if not more, in Balthazar Neumann as in Le Corbusier. Whatever the origins of the tradition, the important point is that it is an immensely fruitful source and one which may also become so for others.

Photographs
Ursula Seitz-Gray

Above: view of the ramp seen from outside: the ramp overlooks the river and the oldest part of the town.
Right: the entry portal looking into the court along the north–south axis.

Left: the central court and its fountain.
Right: view along the linking bridge at
first-floor level towards the Villa Metzler.

Left: the covered link bridge which
connects the new part to the villa which
existed on the site.
Right: the wall opposite the Villa Metzler
is faced in porcelain enamelled panels
and stone slabs.

Left: the pergola in front of the cafeteria
on the west side.
Right: the fountain at the intersection
of two footpaths in the garden on the
west side.

Left: the west side with the cafeteria
terrace.
Right: the east side with offices on the
ground floor.

The south side seen from the carpark.

Left: the bench at the end of the axis in the entrance hall.

Below: the vertical slot which separates the ramp on the right from the galleries on the left.

Top right: the view into the courtyard and the entry into the Chinese galleries on the right on the second floor.

Bottom right: the internal corner at the junction between the Chinese galleries on the left and the link to the third quarter of the museum on the right seen at second-floor level.

Left: looking out from the top of the ramp.
Right: the ramp and the layered walls grading the light to the galleries.

Left: view to the west from
the first floor. On the left, wall-
mounted lights illuminate part
of the reception area below
through the glass roof over the
sales desk.
Right: furniture displays on the
first floor.

Left: showcases and furniture in the Renaissance gallery on the first floor. Right: reading tables in the library on the ground floor.

White walls with window-like openings, hardwood platforms and white walled showcases make up the background to the display. Some of the windows to the exterior have grey woven plastic blinds as above in the 20th century gallery in the display of furniture by Josef Hoffman.

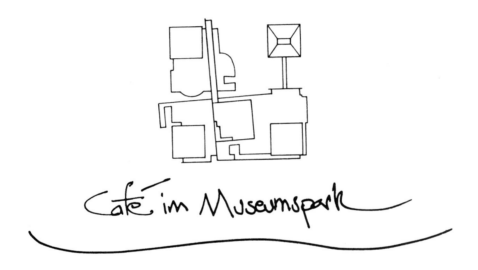

Richard Meier; design for the museum's
café sign and menu cover

Drawings
Oliver Ralphs

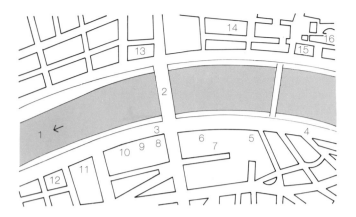

Location plan

1 River Main
2 Untermain Bridge
3 Schaumainkai
4 Sachsenhausener Ufer
5 Museum für Kunsthandwerk
6 Museum of Ethnology – existing
7 Museum of Ethnology – proposed
8 German Film Museum
9 German Architecture Museum
10 German Postal Museum
11 Städel Municipal Gallery
12 Liebieghaus Museum of Culture
13 Jewish Museum
14 Museum of Pre- and Early History
15 Historical Museum
16 Schirn Gallery

Site plan

1 Villa Metzler
2 column on pedestal
3 cafeteria terrace
4 fountain
5 existing Museum of Ethnology

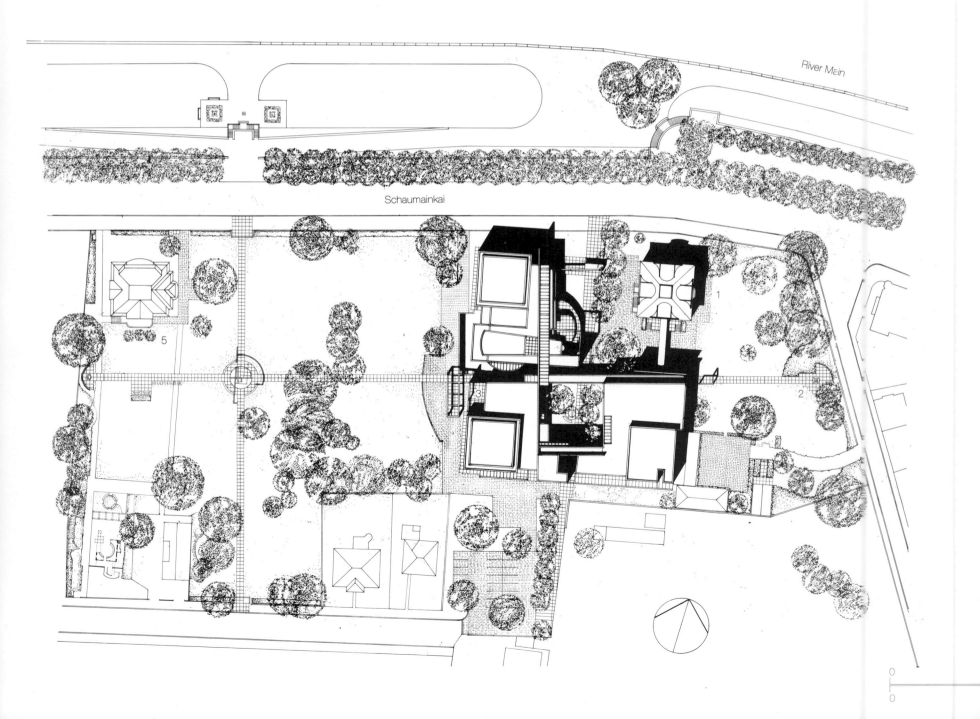

0   500m
0   150feet

Ground-floor plan
1 entrance
2 entrance hall
3 bench
4 sales counter
5 information desk
6 coats
7 gallery for temporary exhibitions
8 ramp to basement and upper
   floors
9 cafeteria
10 kitchen
11 garden court with well
12 library
13 administration
14 Villa Metzler – Rococo galleries

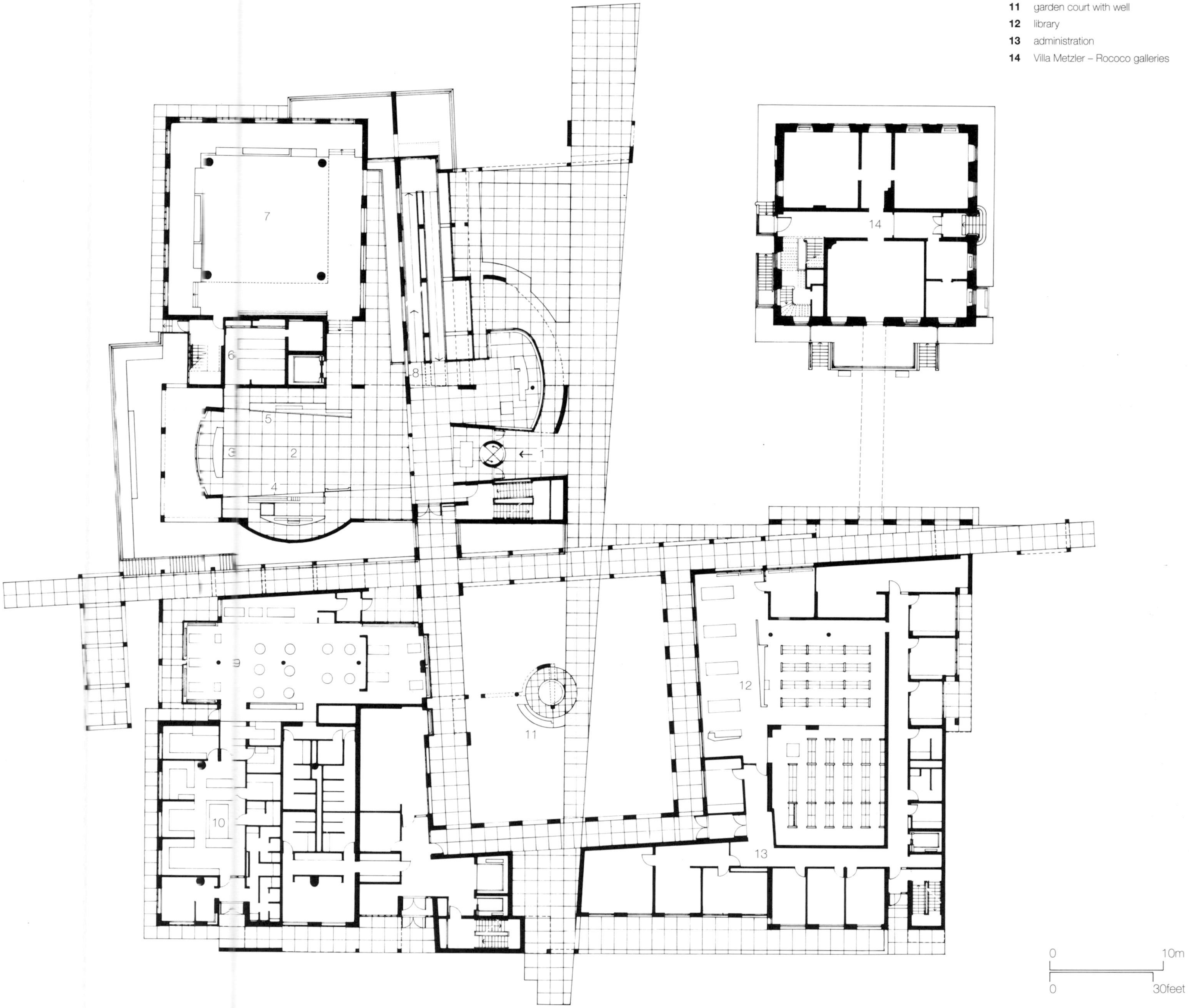

0   10m

0   30feet

First-floor plan
1   20th century
2   19th century
3   Middle Ages
4   Renaissance
5   ramp
6   sitting area
7   terrace
8   Baroque
9   bridge
10 Villa Metzler – Rococo

1

10

7

5

6

2

9

3

8

4

0   10m

0   30feet

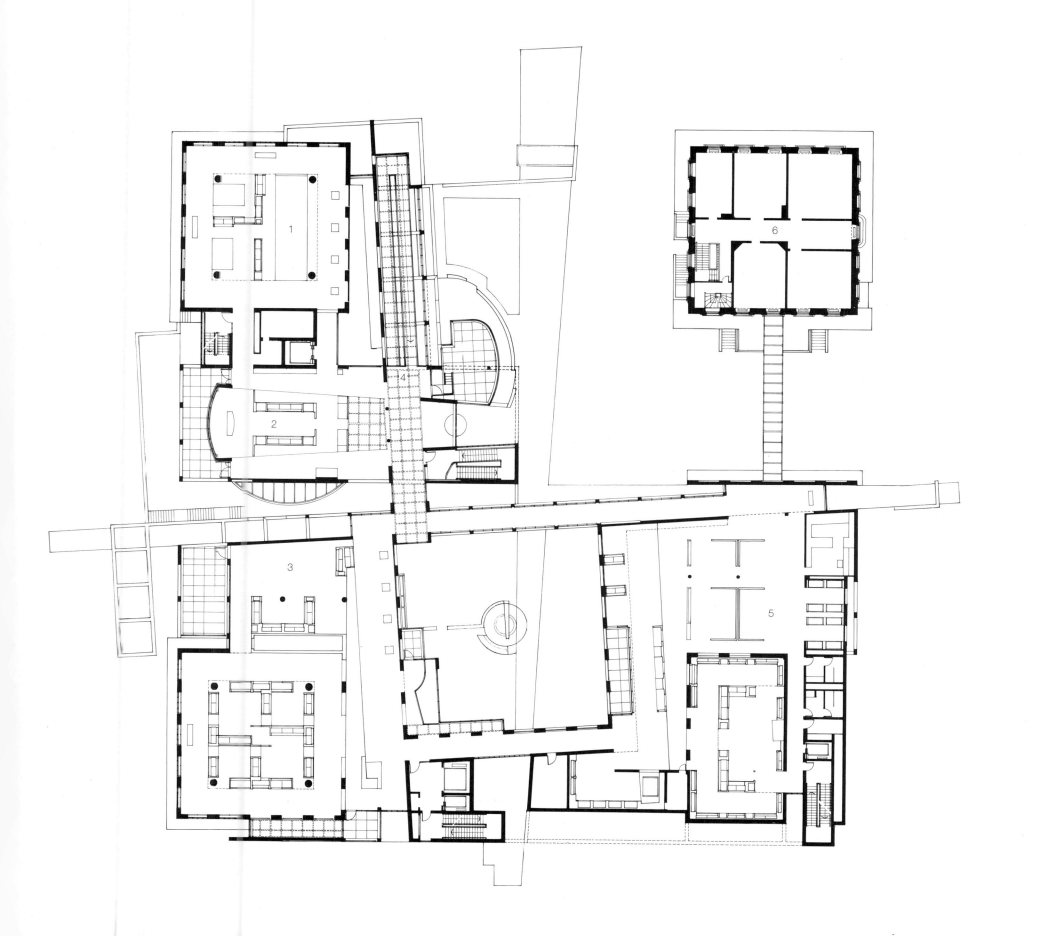

Second-floor plan

1 Persia and India
2 Turkey
3 Far East
4 ramp with glazed roof
5 graphic arts (movable screens)
6 Villa Metzler – Neo-classicism

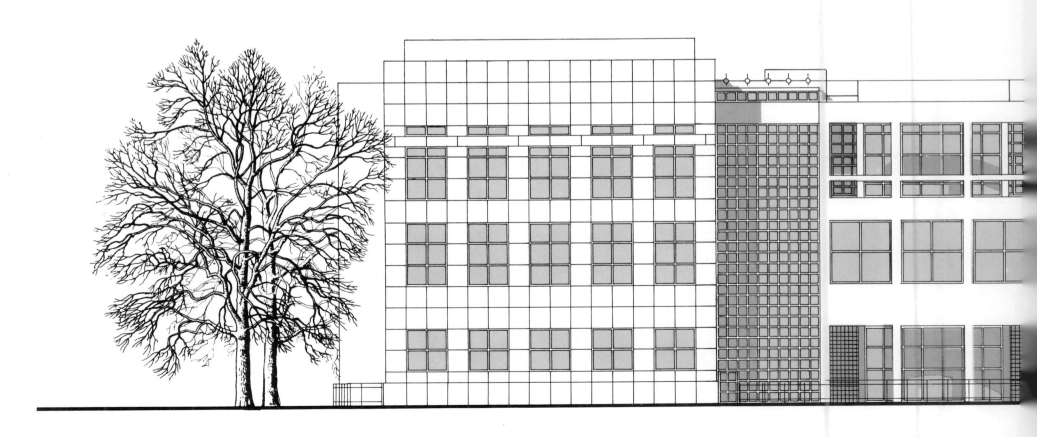

Elevations
Top; elevation facing the river with
Villa Metzler on the left,
Below; elevation to the park; cafeteria
with terrace, centre

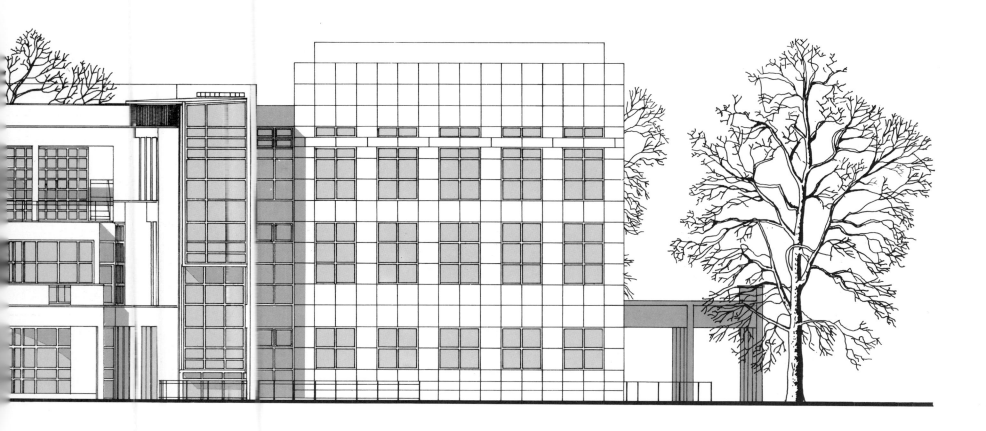

North–south section looking west

1   storage
2   kitchen
3   cafeteria
4   Renaissance
5   Middle Ages
6   Far East
7   plant room
8   walkway with pergola
9   educational section
10 lecture room
11 entrance hall
12 gallery for temporary exhibitions
13 19th century
14 20th century
15 Turkey
16 Persia and India

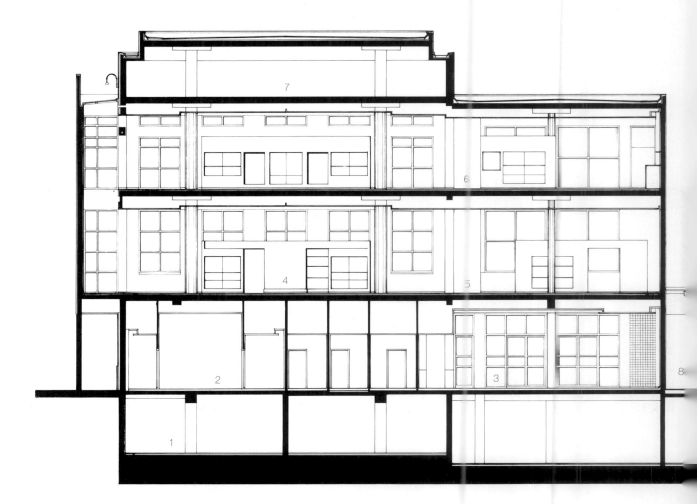

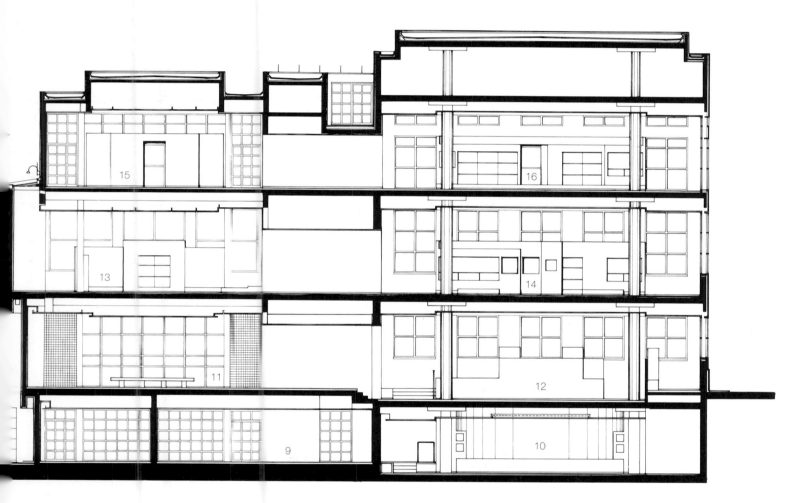

0   10m

0   30feet

Sections

Left; section through ramp looking north
1   air outlet
2   external blind over glazed roof

Right; section through ramp looking west
1   40 × 40mm square mesh panel
2   33mm diameter verticals sleeved
    into 26mm diameter uprights
    welded to steel plate fixed to
    structural concrete
3   26mm diameter horizontal
4   42mm diameter handrail
5   external lighting

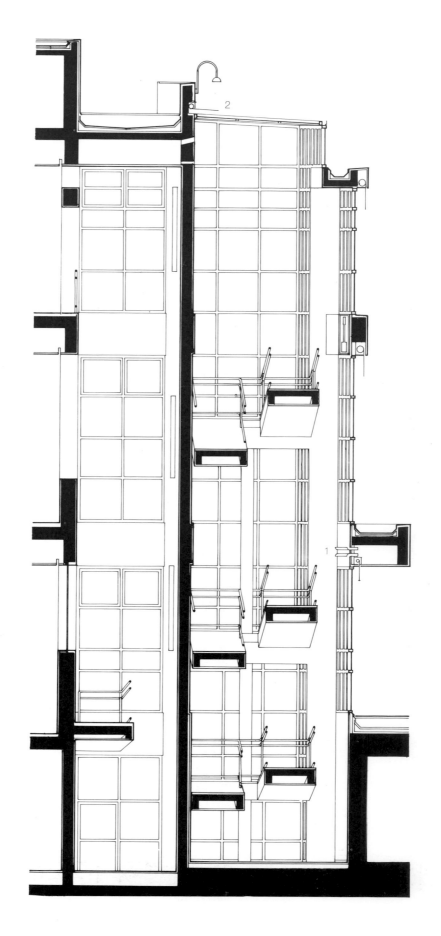

0 ————————————— 5m

0 ————————————— 15feet

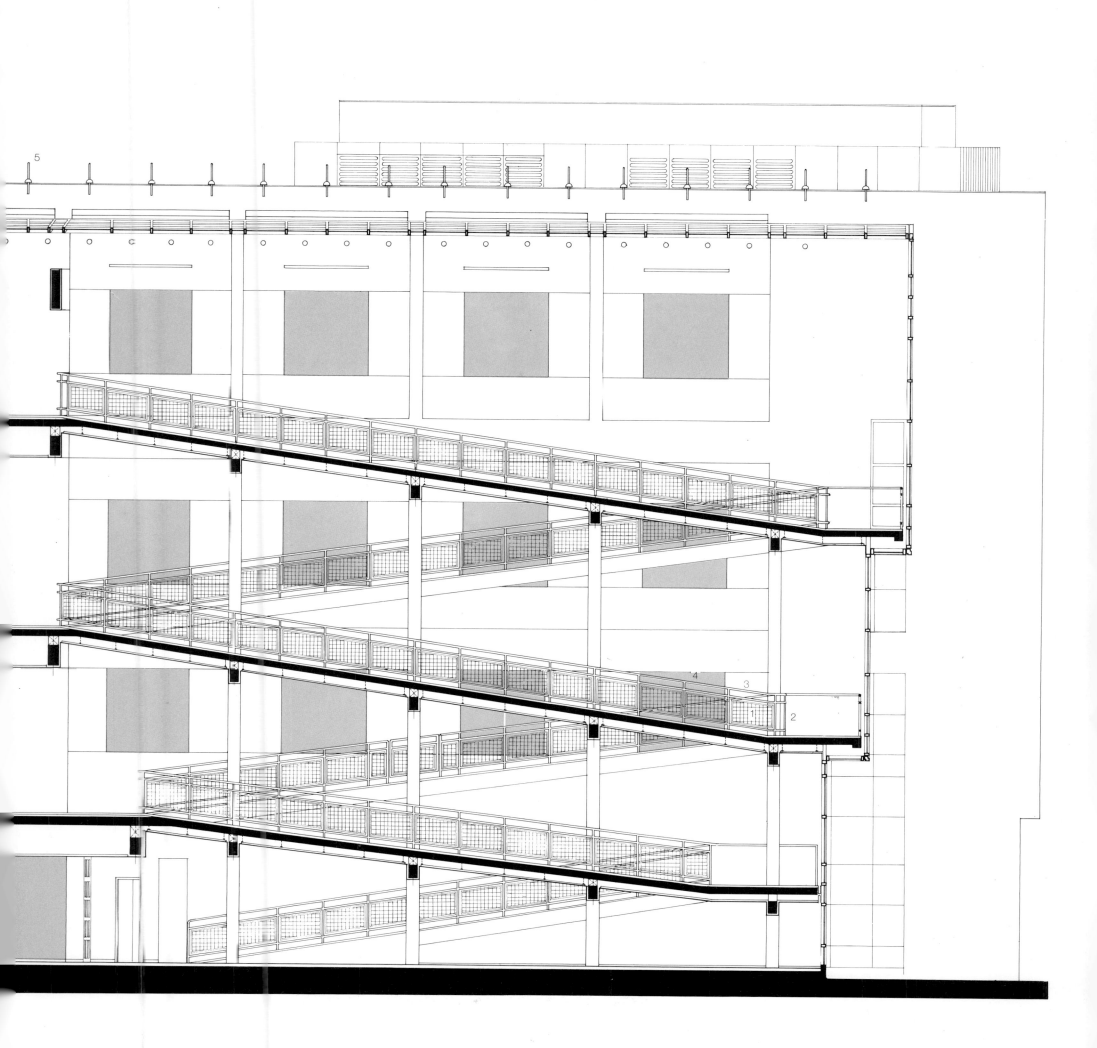

Section through wall opposite the Villa Metzler

1 30mm stone base on stainless steel anchors
2 epoxy jointing
3 15mm internal plaster finish
4 105mm cavity
5 suspended plasterboard ceiling
6 22mm hardwood flooring on screed
7 30mm stone panels hung on stainless steel anchors
8 165mm reinforced concrete
9 250mm reinforced concrete
10 40mm porcelain enamelled panels on stainless steel anchors

Plan sections through porcelain enamelled cladding

1 reinforced concrete
2 7mm gap
3 1.5mm radius
4 40mm porcelain enamelled steel panel
5 stainless steel anchors
6 45mm cavity
7 50mm insulation
8 External corner
9 Internal corner

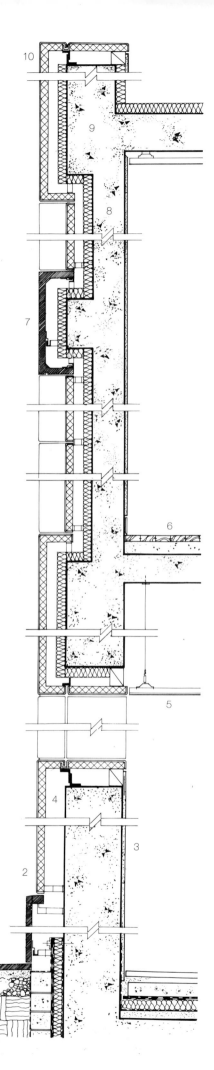

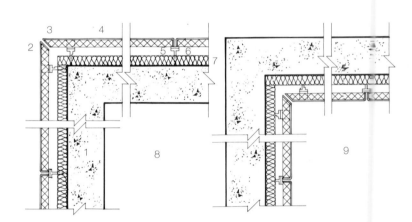

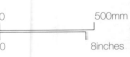

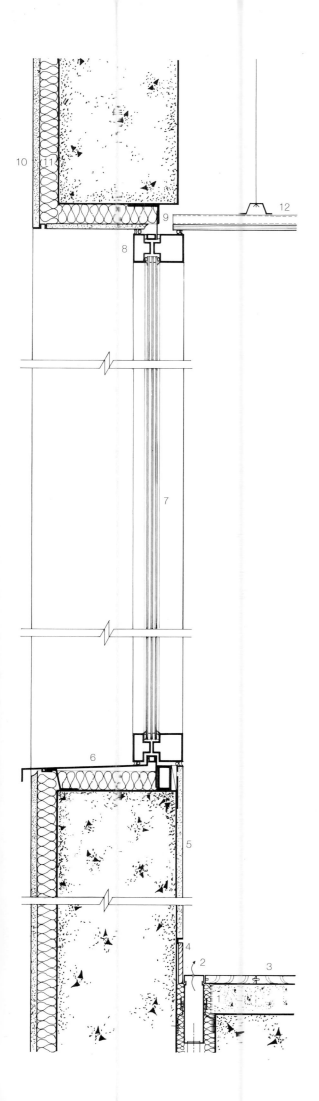

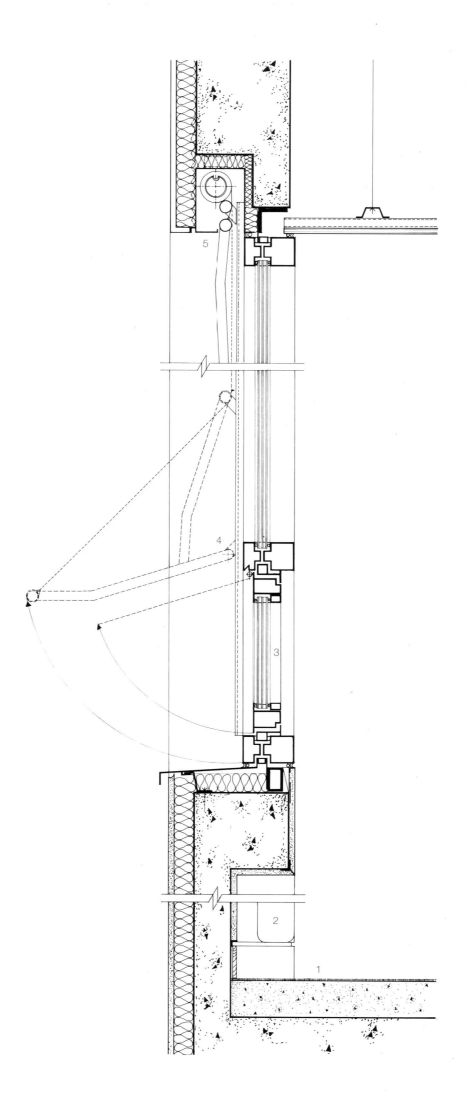

Detailed sections through windows

Left, section through window with
spandrel and floor air outlet

1 mineral wool packing
2 air outlet
3 22mm hardwood floor on screed
4 12mm hardwood skirting
5 15mm internal plaster finish
6 aluminium sill on mastic bedding
7 triple glazing
8 aluminium window with stove enamelled
 finish
9 stainless steel bracket
10 15mm render
11 50mm insulation
12 plasterboard suspended ceiling

Right, section through window with
external sun shading

1 carpet on screed
2 panel type radiator
3 triple-glazed openable window
4 550mm long extension arm for
 external blind
5 aluminium casing for external blind

Section through bridge towards the Villa Metzler

1 stove enamelled metal panel
2 insulation
3 concrete
4 60mm screed with embedded heating elements
5 hardwood floor
6 steel beam
7 radiator
8 fluorescent lighting
9 aluminium sill
10 double glazing
11 aluminium and glass doors
12 internal stiffening rail
13 movable ventilation glass louvres
14 8mm glass, the radius of the glass corresponds to the radius of the window head of the Villa Metzler

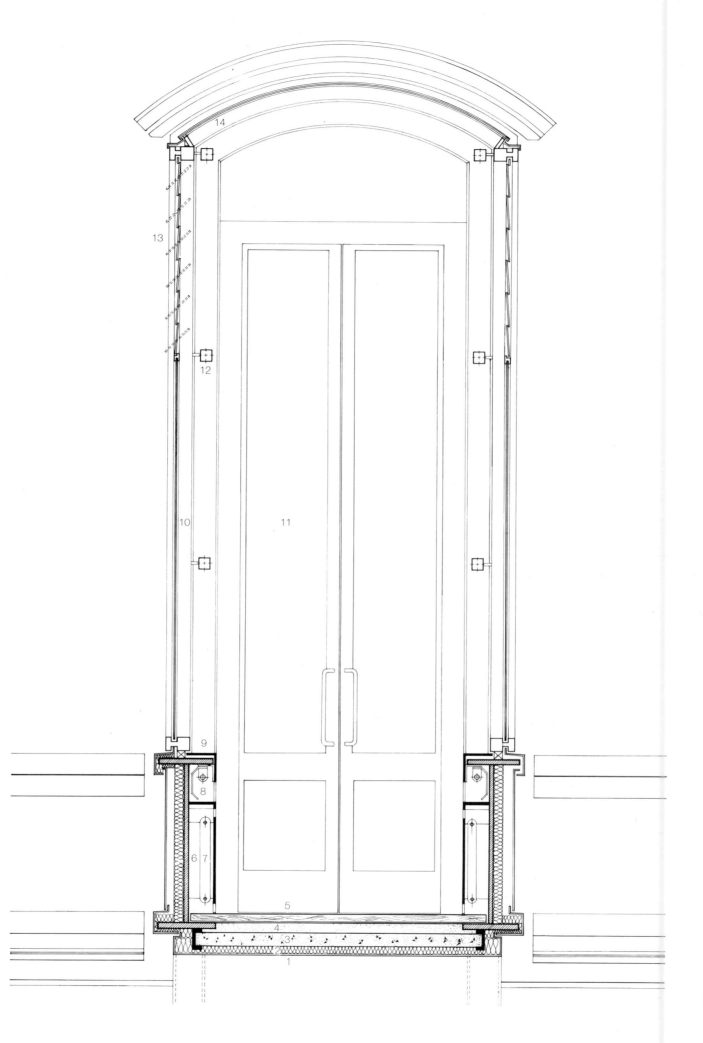

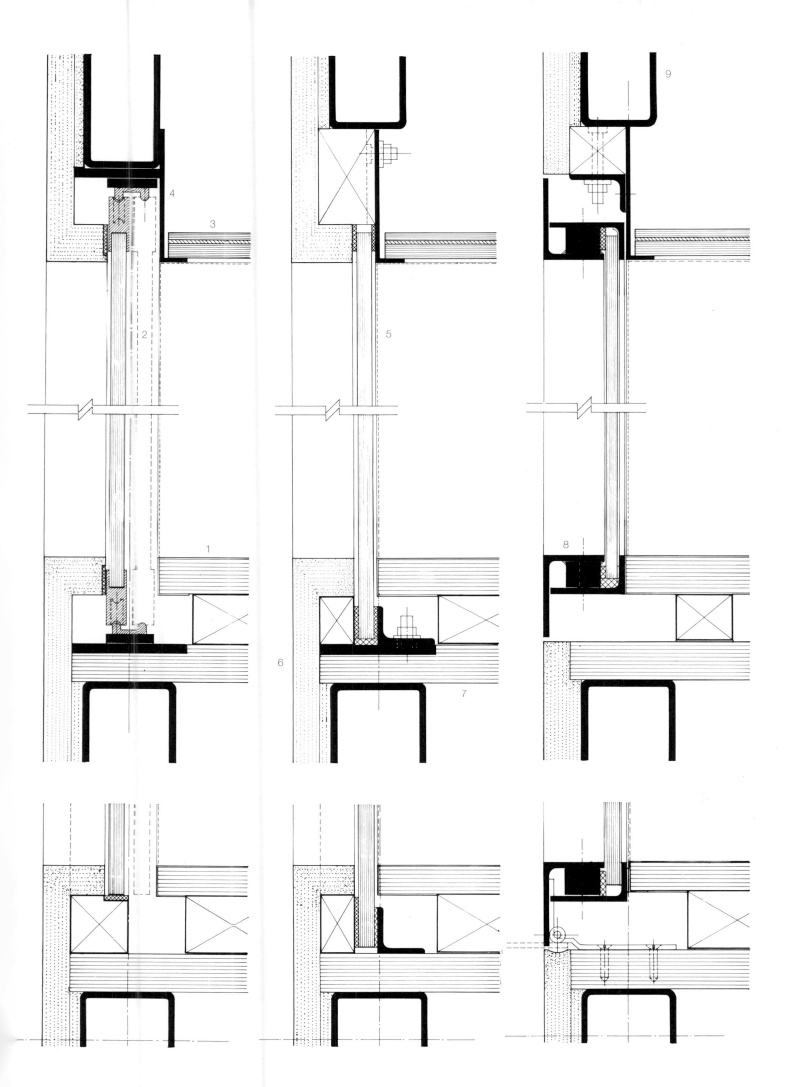

Showcase details

Left; plans and sections of showcase
with sliding glass door
1   fabric-covered plywood
2   sliding glass door
3   'Koolshade' metal louvres and
    ultra-violet filter between two
    sheets of glass with sealed edges
4   steel section

Centre; plan and section of showcase
with fixed glazing
5   fixed glazing
6   particle board on steel and timber
    framing, painted
7   plywood

Right; plan and section of showcase with
framed opening
8   steel section frame, side hung
9   space for fixed and adjustable lighting
    with hinged flap at top for access

Furniture details
This page, information stand in galleries
1100 × 550 × 550mm
1   slots for folding chairs
2   lettering, white on oak stained
    black
3   slots for information sheets

Opposite page; bench
total length 4400mm
1   30 × 30mm hardwood uprights with
    30mm gap
2   oak stained black
3   black leather seat

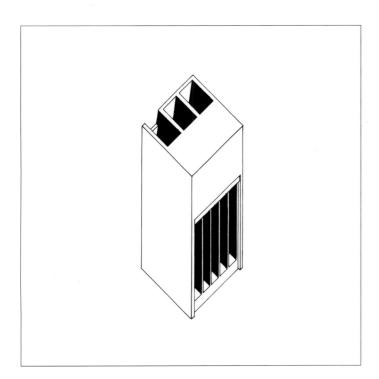

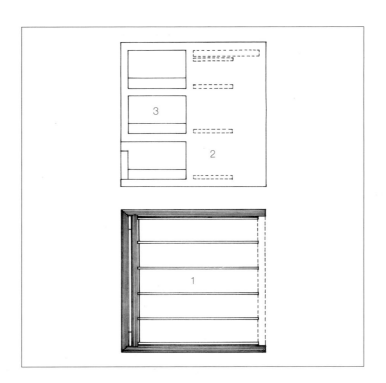

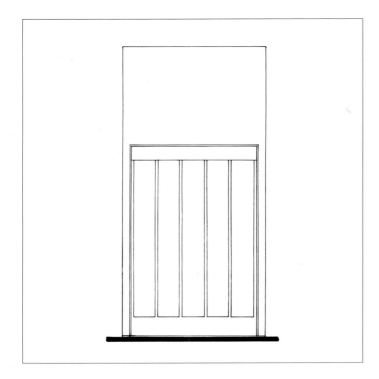

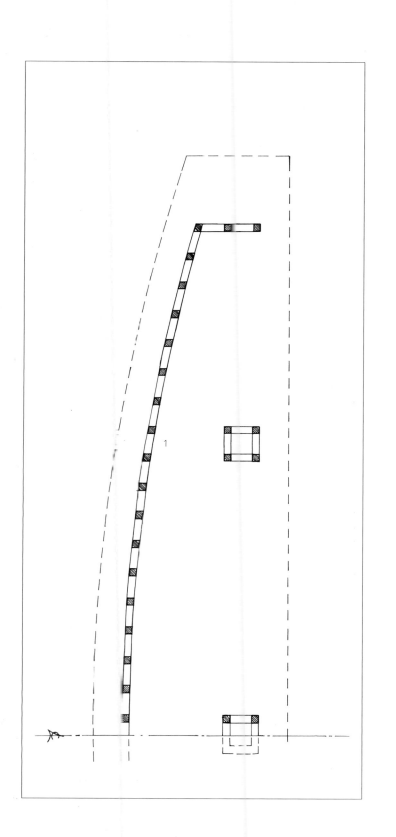

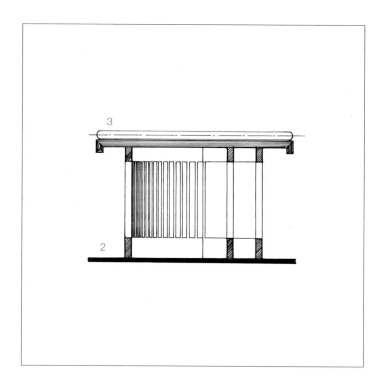

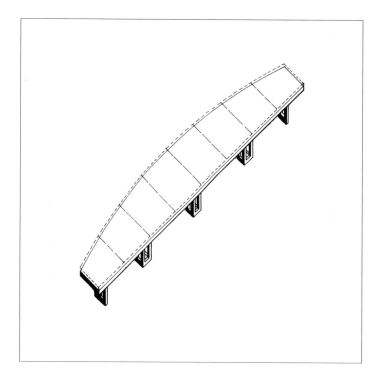

Bibliography

'Architektur: ein "Juwel" für Frankfurt'. *Der Spiegel*, 20 July 1981, 132–134.

'Arts and crafts museum Frankfurt'. *Architectural Review*, October 1980, 196–197.

Blaser, W. *Richard Meier*: Building for Art, Birkhauser Verlag, Basel, 1990, pp. 53–89.

Brenner, D. 'The Frankfurt Museum for the Decorative Arts: theme and variations'. *Architectural Record*, April 1981, 87–95.

Cannon-Brooks, P. 'Frankfurt and Atlanta: Richard Meier as a designer of museums'. *The International Journal of Museum Management and Curatorship*, 5(1), March 1986, 39–64.

Ciriani, H. and Lucan, J. 'Decalages et dynamisme: an interview with Richard Meier' in 'Richard Meier: Museum für Kunsthandwerk'. *AMC*, December 1985, 20–33.

Cobb, H.N. and Meier, R. 'Richard Meier's Museum für Kunsthandwerk'. *Express*, April 1981, 7.

Cook, P. 'White magic'. *Interiors*, July 1985, 202–205, 217–218, 231.

Cook, P. 'Meier Handwerk'. *The Architectural Review*, November 1985, 48–57.

'Crafts museum, Frankfurt'. *Space Design*, February 1986, 29–44.

Dean, A.O. 'Serene, ordered presence in a park'. *Architecture*, January 1986, 56–63.

'Die erste Skizze/the first sketch'. *Daidalos*, 15 September 1982, 46–47.

'Einfach reinlatschen'. *Der Spiegel*, 22 April 1985, 202–207.

Flagge, I. 'Museum für Kunsthandwerk, Frankfurt'. *Lichtbericht*, June 1985, 64–71.

Frampton, K. 'Il museo come mescolanza'. *Casabella*, July/August 1985, 11–17.

Futagawa, Y. (ed.) 'Museum für Kunsthandwerk'. *GA Document* 13, September 1985, 4–41.

Futagawa, Y. 'Winning scheme, Museum for the Decorative Arts Competition, Frankfurt am Main, West Germany'. *Global*, Document 2, 1981, 66–71.

Galloway, D. 'The new German museums'. *Art in America*, July 1985, 74–89.

Galloway, D. 'New museum graces Frankfurt's cultural skyline'. *International Herald Tribune*, 11–12 May 1985, 7.

Goldberger, P. 'New museums harmonize with art'. *The New York Times*, 14 April 1985, sec. 2, 1.

Goldberger, P. 'Harmonizing old and new buildings'. *The New York Times*, 2 May 1985, C23.

Hoyet, J.-M. 'Made in USA: trois conceptions recentes de Richard Meier & Associes'. *Techniques & Architecture*, November 1982, 140–147.

Huse, N. *Richard Meier Museum für Kunsthandwerk, Frankfurt am Main*. Wilhelm Ernst & Sohn Verlag für Architektur und Technische Wissenschaften, Berlin, 1985.

Irace, F. 'Radiant museum'. *Domus*, 662, June 1985, 2–11.

Jaeger, F. 'Schimmernde Perle'. *Deutsche Bauzeitung*, August 1985, 28–33.

Jodidio, P. 'Quand les cathedrales etaient blanches'. *Connaissance des Arts*, July/August 1985, 20.

Klemm, G. 'Museum für Kunsthandwerk'. *Detail*, September/October 1985, 457–466.

Knobel, L. 'Meier's modules'. *Architectural Review*, July 1981, 34–38.

Lampugnani, V. M. 'The jewel with all qualities'. *Lotus International*, 28, 1980, 34–38.

Lampugnani, V.M. *Museumsarchitektur in Frankfurt 1980–1990*, Prestel-Verlag, Munich, 1990, pp. 106–115.

Lemos, P. 'Museum as masterpiece'. *Pan Am Clipper*, September 1985, 57–62.

Lucan, J. 'Le Musée de Francfort: "apprendere à voir l'architecture" 'in 'Richard Meier: Museum für Kunsthandwerk'. *AMC*, December 1985, 20–33.

Maas, T. 'Een Bron van architectonisch Genoegen'. *De Architect*, June 1985, 33.

Montaner, J.M.ª and Oliveras, J. 'Museum of arts and crafts, Frankfurt'. *The Museums of the Last Generation*, Gustavo Gili, S.A., Barcelona, 1986, pp. 102–105.

Murray, P. 'Frankfurt's carbuncle'. *RIBA Journal*, June 1985, 23–25.

'Musée des arts décoratifs, Francfort'. *L'Architecture d'Aujourd'hui*, September 1980, XI–XII.

'Musée de l'artisanat et des metiers d'art Francfort'. *Techniques et Architecture*, April/May 1985, 103–108.

'Museum für Kunsthandwerk'. *Werk, Bauen & Wohnen*, no. 12, December 1984, 36–41.

'Museum für Kunsthandwerk Frankfurt am Main'. *Der Magistrat*, 1985.

'The Museum für Kunsthandwerk'. *A+ U*, September 1985, 15–48.

'Museum für Kunsthandwerk in Frankfurt'. *Baumeister*, August 1980, 767–773.

'Museum für Kunsthandwerk in Frankfurt'. *Baumeister*, August 1985, 22–33.

'Neue Tempel für die Kunst'. *Stern*, 25 April 1985, 46–66.

Papadakis, A. (ed.) 'Richard Meier a personal manifesto', 'Museum for the Decorative Arts, Frankfurt, West Germany'. *Architectural Design*, 55(1/2), 1985, 56, 58–69.

Rumpf, P. 'Museum für Kunsthandwerk, Frankfurt am Main'. *Bauwelt*, May 1985, 766–777.

Ruthenfranz, E. 'Nobler Kulter-Park für die Burger.' *Art, das Kunstmagazin*, September 1983, 68–74.

Sabisch, C. 'Kein Manhattan in "Manhattan"'. *Der Apotheker*, July 1985, 5.

Schilgen, J. *Neue Hauser für die Kunst*, Harenberg Kommunikation, Dortmund, 1990, pp. 82–105.

Schreiber, M. 'Weisses Bauhaus Schloss'. *Frankfurter Allgemeine Zeitung*, 27 April 1985.

Stephens, S. 'Frame by frame'. *Progressive Architecture*, June 1985, 81–91.

'Ten star museums: white on white'. *Monografias de Arquitectura y Vivienda*, no. 18, 1989, 57–63.

Van Dijk, H. 'Richard Meier in Duitsland: Museum für Kunsthandwerk, Frankfort'. *Wonen Tabk*, 15 July 1985, 20–28.

Werner, F. 'Der wettbewerb für das Museum für Kunsthandwerk in Frankfurt am Main' in *Jahrbuch für Architektur: Neues Bauen 1980–1981* (ed. H. Klotz), 1981, pp. 22–29, 30–39.

Wilson, W. 'Germany's grand designs'. *The Los Angeles Times*, 3 November 1985, 74–77.

Zardini, M. 'Il Bianco e Il Grigio'. *Casabella*, July/August 1985, 1–10.

Credits

Client: City of Frankfurt
Architects: Richard Meier & Partners,
    New York
Design Team: Richard Meier, Günter
    R. Standke, Michael Palladino
Project partner: Günter R. Standke
Collaborators: Hans Goedeking, John
    Eisler, Manfred Fischer, David
    Diamond, Margaret Bemiss,
    Geoffrey Wooding
Construction and financial
    management:
building: Frankfurter Aufbau AG
    (FAAG), Frankfurt
interior: City of Frankfurt
Structural engineering: G.
    Rosenboom, Frankfurt
Structural engineering review and
    time scheduling:
    Ingenieursocietät BGS,
    Frankfurt
Building physics: Planungsbüro
    Dr Gruschka, Bensheim
Soil engineering: Kleiner & Warko,
    Frankfurt
Acoustics: Professor K. Weisse,
    Frankfurt
Heating, ventilating, air conditioning
    and water engineering:
    Pettersson & Ahrens, Ober-
    Mörlen
Electrical engineering and lighting:
    A. Zitnik, Frankfurt
Elevator engineering: W. Futterer,
    Wiesbaden
Exterior wall consultants: Institute for
    Facade Technology, Frankfurt
Surveyors: City of Frankfurt

Chronology

November 1979–April 1980
    Competition held
October 1980–December 1981
    Design period
March 1982–April 1985
    Construction (building and
    museum installation)
25 April 1985
    Opening

Statistics

Areas
Exhibition 4800m^2
Villa Metzler 879m^2
Temporary exhibitions 360m^2
Administration 314m^2
Lecture hall 300m^2
Cafeteria 330m^2
Teaching 380m^2
Storage 535m^2
Workshops 400m^2
Library 370m^2
Enclosed volume 61,141m^3
Cost in 1985 DM 43,521,000

Awards

1986 American Institute of Architects
New York Chapter – Honor Award
1987 American Institute of Architects
National Chapter – Honor Award

Richard Meier has also been awarded
the following:
1980 American Institute of Architects
New York Chapter – Medal of Honor
1984 Pritzker Architecture Prize
1988 Royal Institute of British
Architects Gold Medal

List of works

1961–62	House for Mr and Mrs Saul Lambert, Fire Island, New York	1969	Charles Evans Industrial Buildings, State University College, Fredonia, New York, New York State Construction Fund	1971	Dormitory for the Olivetti Training Center, Tarrytown, New York, Olivetti Corporation of North America
1963	Exhibition design and organization 'Recent American Synagogue Architecture', The Jewish Museum New York, New York		Charles Evans Industrial Buildings, Fairfield, New Jersey, and Piscataway, New Jersey	1971–76	House for Mr and Mrs Richard Maidman, Sands Point, New York House for Mr and Mrs James Douglas, Jr, Harbor Springs, Michigan
1963–65	House for Mr and Mrs Jerome Meier, Essex Fells, New Jersey		Bronx Redevelopment Planning Study, New York City Housing and Development Administration and The New York City Planning Commission	1972	East Side Housing, New York, New York (with Emery Roth Architects), Tishman Reality, and Construction Corporation
1964	Monumental Fountain Competition, Benjamin Franklin Parkway, Philadelphia, Pennsylvania (with Frank Stella)		House in Pound Ridge, Pound Ridge, New York	1972–74	House for Mr and Mrs Stuart Shamberg, Mount Kisco, New York
1964–65	Studio and apartment for Frank Stella, New York, New York		Robert R. Young Housing, New York, New York, General Properties Corporation	1973	Paddington Station Housing, New York, New York A Museum of Modern Art, Villa Strozzi, Florence, Italy, The Commune of Florence
1964–66	House for Professor and Mrs Arch Dotson, Ithaca, New York Renfield House, Chester, New Jersey (with Elaine Lustig Cohen)	1969–71	House in Old Westbury, Old Westbury, New York Twin Parks Northeast Housing, Bronx,	1974	Condominium Housing, Yonkers, New York, H. Development Corporation Cornell University Undergraduate Housing, Ithaca, New York
1965	University Arts Center Competition, University of California, Berkeley, California (with John Hejduk and Robert Slutzky) Rubin Loft Renovation, New York, New York	1969–72	New York, New York State Urban Development Corporation Monroe Development Center,	1975	Commercial Building and Hotel, Springfield, Massachusetts, Mondev International Corporation Wingfield Racquet Club, Greenwich,
1965–67	House for Mr and Mrs Fred Smith, Darien, Connecticut	1969–74	Rochester, New York (with Todd and Giroux, Associates Architects), Facilities Development Corporation for the New York State Department of Mental Hygiene		Connecticut, H. Development Corporation The Theatrum, New Harmony, Indiana, Historic New Harmony Inc.
1965–76	'Sona' Shop for the Handicrafts and Handlooms, Exports Corporation of India, New York, New York, (with Elaine Lustig Cohen)	1970–77	Bronx Development Center, Bronx, New York, Facilities Development Corporation for the New York State Department of Mental Hygiene	1975–78	Warehouse Rehabilitation for the Bronx Psychiatric Center, Bronx, New York, Facilities Development Corporation for the New York State Department of Mental Hygiene
1966	Mental Health Facilities, West Orange, New Jersey, Jewish Counceling and Service Agency	1971	Olivetti Branch Office prototype, Irvine, California; Kansas City, Missouri; Minneapolis, Minnesota; Boston, Massachusetts; Brooklyn, New York;		Pottery Shed for the Robert Lee Blaffer Trust, New Harmony, Indiana, Mrs Kenneth Dale Owen
1966–67	House for Mr and Mrs David Hoffman, East Hampton, New York		Patterson, New Jersey; Olivetti Corporation of North America Modification of the Branch office	1975–79	The Atheneum, New Harmony, Indiana, Historic New Harmony Inc.
1967–70	Westbeth Artists' Housing, Greenwich Village, New York, New York, J.M. Kaplan Fund and The National Council on the Arts		Prototype, Riverside, California; Albuquerque, New Mexico; Tuscon, Arizona; Fort Worth, Texas; Portland,	1976	Alamo Plaza, Colorado Springs, Colorado Mondev International Corporation
1967–69	House for Mr and Mrs Renny Saltzman, East Hampton, New York		Maine; Memphis, Tennessee; Roanoke, Virginia; Olivetti Corporation of North America		
1968	Health and Physical Education Building, State University College, Fredonia, New York, New York State Construction Fund				